Conceptions

Picas Series 9

JANE DICK

Conceptions

Guernica

Montreal, 1992

Some of the poems contained herein have previously appeared in
Los, The Alchemist, Grain, and *Inland Sea*. I wish to thank
Antonio for his unfailing support and for his perseverance.

Printed in Canada.
Typesetting by Mégatexte, Montréal.
Published for the first time in this format in 1992.
Cover photograph by Barry Pask.

Antonio D'Alfonso, editor.
Guernica Editions Inc.
P.O. Box 633, Station N.D.G.
Montréal (Québec), Canada H4A 3R1.

Dépot légal — 3e trimestre
Bibliothèque nationale du Québec
& National Library of Canada.

Canadian Cataloguing in Publication Data
Dick, Jane, 1952-
Conceptions

(Pica series ; 9)
Poems.
ISBN 0-920717-49-7

I. Title. II. Series.

PS8557.I254C63 1992 C811'.54 C91-090026-4
PR9199.3.D43C63 1992

Contents

KALEIDOSCOPE

CONCEPTIONS

For A.

KALEIDOSCOPE

Exquis

the first syllable of your name
bursts from me
like a birthing cry

my lips run breathless
with its sound
like fingers over skin

your touch
gives tongue to silences
inside me you are music

i am filled
with the exquisite stillness
of your body
briefly held
intense, soaring

pleasure wells in me
like a fountain
flesh cascades over flesh

your smell alone
satisfies more senses
than my body can desire

I Am Astonished

i am astonished
as i emerge
each time
from the cocoon
of our sheets

to see your body
stretching magnificently
like a lion
like Da Vinci's man
in the wheel

the muscles
of your torso
excite me
tense and ready
stretching
rising gloriously
like a sun

stretching in the morning
filling the room
your arms
your thighs quiver
with the pleasure
of the strain

your body is a rushing wind
that laughs
at our cocoon
and dares
my wings to dry

it encloses the day
and releases
the day
and the time
the suns
the rushing winds
the wings
of all my butterflies

you stand
exhilarating
free

though you stretch
each morning
it is always
unprecedented
surprising

i am refreshed
and astonished
every time

I Could Not Lock My Door

i could not lock my door
against your clean body
so i painted it shut with spittle
i built a house of liquid
fluid
fluid
it spilled its walls
and trickled through
the cracks in your skin

Limbo

we can feel the circle
grinning viciously in the darkness.
yet we come together
as far from the centre
as far from the circumference
it takes only our time
and part of our lives —
nothing really.
lonely
we come together
and in the coming together
reach the climax of our loneliness.
still we haven't the courage
to be alone
alone.
it's too dark.
we need to hear a body's touch
say we're not alone.
we smile ah, we are together;
ah, we are
an illusion of not alone.
still we come together
we can feel the circle
              we can't find the exits
grinning viciously in the darkness.

Kaleidoscope

kisses
spinning like colours in a dream
bodies
milky crystal fountains
falling up through memories falling up

you and i
are the us that came before
that follows after
always the same, never the same
like giddy snowflakes in mid-May

drunk with brandy
swimming in champagne
living in the bubbles' fragile vintage

mad idiots dancing in an hourglass, we
(the us that came before, and after)
the sand rushing through
its liquid brilliance,
strange sacrifice to joy

turning turning our little lives
faster faster to cease the spinning
to hold the shadow of a kiss
to capture a single pattern

watching through a small round hole
the dizzy pieces gone berserk
a silent movie of the us
that always is and never was;
no piano playing, just the click
of pieces tumbling in a prism.

                              fools are we who bathe in wine
                              and watch it flow like blood
                              through grasping fingers

J.H.D.

your hair lies
tired across the pillow
dreamlessly remembering
the nights before

fingers frantically
running through
caresses
like piano scales

waltzing
through your hair
tying knots with each left hand
(always the left)
until you drew your sword
and split the knots

the blood flowed
frantically
like fingers
through your hair

you were up all night
performing transfusions
until your hair flowed
in the injured veins

exhausted
(you never meant to be a surgeon)
the sweat has dried on your brow
your worn-out hair
lies weeping on the pillow

For Kenny

Kenny, going to Wembley
whoever you are,
i'd like to be with you.
you're gentle, half asleep,
i think we were sad on the train
(we were soft in the darkness)
playing mother to your lover
                    playing child
soft my skin so soft
your mouth so soft …
Kenny, gone to Wembley
whoever you are —
Cheerio,
and i hope you win the game.

My Breasts Want You

my breasts want you
so intensely
they lift my body skyward
nipples burning like suns

clamouring for your fiery tongue
storms flood my veins
my skin howls
my breasts carry me
to the heart of desire

i am hollow and full
i cannot hold you more tightly
than this

About the Dog

for 'Sam'

was gonna write a poem
about the dog
watching us make love
but Michael Ondaatje already did

about the dog
running nails clacking
across the bedroom floor
noble dog to the rescue
of the moaning lady
puzzled, finds his master
smiling
and retires to his corner
one eye open, just in case

about the dog
afterwards
coming to the bed for comfort
resting his chin
on my thigh,
blinking,
whimpering puppy sounds

Beside You

there are times when
just waking beside you
is all the pleasure
i can contain

Postscript

it surprises me
when our desires have been met
i lie like a crucifix
you resting on my back
my hands reach the edges of the bed
my head wishes
                    to fall to the floor

My Breasts Are Made of Brass

my breasts are made of brass
they *cring*
like cymbals
flattened sterile cones
responding to your beat
relentlessly
    crashing down

i haven't your rhythm
i would crash
    in mid-
    beat

then you'd replace me,
melt down the brass
for an ash-
    tray

The First Whiff of Smoke

i lay there
after you'd gone
just as you'd left me
vulnerable
yet you spoke to me
as you stood in the doorway
as though —
as though i was fully clothed
and sitting across the table.
You know,
you said,
I can smell burning in the hall.
and i knew we would all be consumed.

I Will No Longer

i will no longer speak of you.
here, it is so

                      precarious

on the cliff's
edge
a whisper
could snowball
into something altogether too big,
clearing my throat
could crumble
this last ledge of dust
and leave us
gaping
in-
to
the canyon.

Gazebo

you built une tour d'Eiffel
out of toothpicks
(i recall it was the rage)
such devotion
you gave
to those tiny sticks
until they stood
and surveyed a tiny Paris
of dust
upon my dresser.

between my fingers
they broke so easily
(! my fingers are so small —)
every single stick
snapped
and your spinning body
spun a thousand times
down down
to the debris
in the dusty streets of Paris.

'this—' you said,
as you traced a finger
through the rubble
'was the Champs Elysée,
and this —'
was the way you cleared the tiny broken sticks
and the dust,
sweeping all of Paris to the floor.

on my clean dresser now
you can build again
monsieur,
with your toothpicks,
a gazebo
for me
where i can write this poem.

Reflections

the mirror squints
distorting the reflections
the images
that rip-ripple-rippled
on our private ponds

we tossed our moments
like horseshoes
forever thudding in the dust
forever like blind archers
missing the target
losing our arrows
in forgotten haystacks
in forgotten golden fields

we ran like tumbleweeds
tumbled like young animals
old lovers
trapped in the loft
afraid of broken ladder rungs

afraid of breaking mirrors
— but we did —
and now
the mirror squints
for it
like us
forgets the blow
that distorted the reflections

I Hear You Knocking

often at night
i wake
i hear you knocking

i don't answer
i'm so afraid
you won't be there

When the Bleeding Stops

when the bleeding stops
i'll sit quietly
cutting cancer dressings
from our sheets.

as soon as we know
which of us is the patient
one of us will die;
it will be an act of mercy.

Trees

there are days
the trees kneel
and kiss me
there are times
they hold my limbs
and carry me
through the forest
gently gently
with the joy of growing things

times there are
the trees dance
to their winds
and i to mine

sometimes
the trees do not bend
they beckon
come hither
from inflexible boughs

these moments
stability is cold

strength is bitter
when the trees do not bend
all that they gave me
withers and falls

i love to dance
in the forest
but i cannot trust the trees

Release

i will take a thousand
flying photographs
of you —
towering over me, or
lost in sleep,
your jaw slack

the shower spray sparkling
on your flattened hairs
clinging to your wet
body like small animals
hanging on
to something solid

you standing in the kitchen
with a knife intent
on your chopping
chopping
we are out of matches and
you do not mind

chewing on a stray
moustache hair
lost in your teeth

the final roll of film
will catch you running
to the window
hair flying for freedom
raging at the drapes that will
not part
tearing through the singing
glass away from the
darkroom thousands

that picture i will
take flying with me
every
where

Exploratory

in the hands of the unskilled surgeon
the knife soars too deeply

carving uncertain patterns
designed to heal
he knows not what

unqualified to judge
the patient lies stunned
awaiting the stroking of the knife
like a caress

folding the running blood
between the hands
and holding them up
for analysis

CONCEPTIONS

Inception

need tumbled from her lips
like silence

falling into crevices
she had not foreseen

he opened his body
like a seed
and planted her with words

what does this mean?
asked the reapers

i do not know
she said, growing,
he is as silent as blood

She Laboured Long

She laboured long with her burden
did Time,
simultaneous
with conception
she strove
        gently
                urgently
                        frantically

pushing out the Life

a difficult birth
at fall of night
the gravedigger took the forceps

having no choice

sweet blind Pozzo
bloody deaf and dumb
came screaming
for a moment
in the light.

giving birth
astride a grave
of course
the child fell in.

                wrapped in cozy sod,
                satisfied —
                You did just fine, Mother.

Elusive

sometimes i wish
i could hold your child in me
(a tangible proof that you exist)

each time i conceive with you
the little foreign object
in my womb
discards our child
like an unfertilized egg

as elusive as you
i've never seen them
— the eggs, the children —
never touched them
never borne their pain

how many of our unwanted children
slipped away silently,
how many might have stayed?

i'd like to hold them
— just this once

Mirror

mirror,
i've been staring into you
like a hungry child
in a magazine ad
belly distended
       with the unborn
       the undead

i don't know when
my belly began to swell
one of those nights
when you didn't roll over
on your side
one of those nights
when i thought we'd
reached through the hunger

but it's growing in me now

the growing doesn't interest you
flatly you watch it
your passion
dissipates like air

something has to matter

your dinner
the crease in your trousers
my squirming like a grub
under the white light
       of your returned stare

we undead are struggling
it's too late to be unborn

Eggs Break

eggs break
fall through my hands

stare up from the floor
pale
translucent as embryos

tenderly scooped
they cling to my fingers
unfertilized and sad

cool as semen
cool as corpses
slithering down my gullet
greedy for death

one raw second

Empty Shells

my own fallopian tubes
are petrified

i let you in
one green and poisoned night
molten lava sperm
tails of fire, heads of ash

my eggs since birth
began to ooze
and boil with rotting

phantom eggs now
their death comforts you
a sense of history welds us
we are in this together

> i erupt sometimes
> over breakfast bacon
> keenly despise its fat
> i think of you burning

lack of possibility
sucks me like a weasel
lack of choice
wastes me like disease

for the hardening
of my main arteries
there is no forgiveness

> while you shower and shave
> eggs crack
> on the pan's edge
> cast-iron
>
> > my guts
>
> i sizzle
> the eggs fry

Anomaly

i like to think
i once carried your child in me
i would wake in the night
my belly black and blue
beating on it like a drum
bashing its brains out

Child Images

I

there are children playing
outside my door
scrabbling at the wood
chattering busily

II

little children picking scabs
gleeful watch their own
fascinated blood
bubble painlessly forth

III

a woman on the bus
carried a dead child
i remember the blue jacket
and the white boots buckled
so neatly

Ile Bizard, Bord du Lac

can you imagine these children
in the pool, splashing
the white spray
up like fans, and foamy
can you imagine their pleasure
this still song-filled night
a dog barking
the birds
a giggling that might be the children
or the water

my vision is patterned
by strands of hair
falling as i turn my head
and smile
and follow another joyous dive
another fan of spray

i am outside in
what must be a symphony
the song within me
is bursting into
silence
splashing me with incoherence

i must go inside now
and assemble
these sensations
into a comparable embrace

June 1975

Warriors

Hector, three years old
when i first held him

Hector of the infected ear
(confession:
i never cleaned it)
Hector of the complete lack
of understanding of where he was
of who the adults were
entering, leaving his life
(seven hour shifts:
we called this children's aid)
Hector, yet too young
for war's monotonies
learned anyway

canned food, no toothbrush
one change of clothes
yelling never ceased

there were too many boys
in the place

children,
they shouldered adult anguish
hearts harder than fists
unspecified fears made them brothers
animal instinct left them foes

the older boys threw knives like glances
wielded broken bottles, tin can lids
sticks, stones

mixed blood ran like frightened prey
over battered limbs
teeth and fingers lost in battles
— nothing won, war a habit

Hector, only three
cries into my skirts
(present tense:
he haunts me)
he mourns a vague mother
locked somewhere for something
snot bubbles through his nostrils
(this place we called a home
out of kleenex again)
powerless to heal, i hold him

Hector, very small, and shrinking
buried in chaos, breaks away
hurtles headlong into battle
his pain a boundless rage

(Hector was a famous warrior
loved and honoured in triumphant death)
Hector was a warrior indeed
he knew nothing of Trojans
had no need of mythologies
Hector was a warrior

older now, he is
still three in my mind
and perceives himself dying
as children can, and do

unprepared for his war cries
(they trouble my sleep)
echoing through our shared history:
Hector, only three
mourns his birth

Child, or Lack of

child, or lack of
child
come here
eye of my storm
salvation
answer to swollen days
flower my rocky flesh

no, there is no hearing
in this tempest
my blood pounding in your ears

child, go away
do not come
heart of my anguish
these walls have all they can
to hold themselves

they are intact now
though fragile

i am not for mothering
yet no birthing tears me
so harshly as choice
wanting or loathing you
there is no explaining
let me ache in peace, child
you will not come
this choice is mine

child, or lack of
child
close your eyelids
translucent over me